T0069146

1595

Fallen from a Chariot

Books by Kevin Prufer

Strange Wood
The Finger Bone
Fallen from a Chariot

Fallen from a Chariot

Kevin Prufer

Carnegie Mellon University Press
Pittsburgh 2005

Acknowledgments

Agni: "Roman Economics"; *Boulevard:* "In the End the Doorbells Stop," "Youth and the Lie That Goes with It," "Old Woman," "Dissected Bird," "An Angel"; *Boston Review:* "Underground Mausoleum"; *Epoch:* "Beautiful Nero," "The Empire in the Air," "Poor Hannibal of Carthage," "Lives of the Later Caesars"; *Field:* "The Rise of Rome," "Caligula, Clairvoyant," "Claudius Adrift"; *Free Verse:* "Lily"; *Green Mountains Review:* "Ode to Rome"; *Hawaii Pacific Review:* "The Dead in Their Boats"; *Jacket:* "For the Dead"; *The Journal:* "Burial at Sea"; *Kenyon Review:* "Questions for the Drowned at Sea"; *Lit:* "About the Dead," "For the Dead: Unveiling"; *Literary Imagination:* "My Life with Caesar"; *Mid-American Review:* "Apocalyptic Prayer," "I Was the Last Man on Earth"; *Natural Bridge:* "The Death of Augustus,"; *New England Review:* "Fallen from a Chariot," "An Ambulance"; *Notre Dame Review:* "Goodbye to the City, We Have No Other," "The Fall of Rome"; *Ploughshares:* "The Fall of the Roman Empire"; *Prairie Schooner:* "They Shall Be Left to Fall as They Are Inclined by Their Own Weight," "Prayer"; *River City:* "Caligula on Death"; *Shade:* "The Fall of Rome," "Air Disaster Over Kansas"; *Slope:* "Narcissistic Elegy," "Lemure"; *The Southwest Review:* "Final Instructions"; *Verse:* "A Car Has Fallen from a Bridge," "For the Dead"; *Washington Square:* "Poem for My Mother at Her Age"; *Willow Springs:* "Who Are Our Barbarians?"

"Beautiful Nero" was reprinted in the 2004 *Pushcart Prize Anthology*, edited by Bill Henderson. Several of these poems were also awarded the George Bogin Memorial Award of the Poetry Society of America. "Lily" received the Emily Dickinson Prize of the Poetry Society of America. "The Gladiator" was printed as a special, limited-edition broadside as part of the Underwood Poetry Broadside Series, edited by Kent Shaw and Jason Stumpf. "Questions for the Drowned at Sea" was reprinted as a fine press chapbook designed by Ellen Sheffield for the *Kenyon Review* Poets Series.

Thanks to Mary Hallab, Joy Katz, R. M. Kinder, Wayne Miller, Alan Michael Parker, Molly Peacock, and J. D. Smith for their insights and criticism.

On the cover: "Corona Del Mar" by Mell Killpatrick.
© Jennifer Dumas Collection.

Library of Congress Control Number: 2003112553
ISBN 0-88748-423-9
ISBN 0-88748-419-0 Pbk.

Copyright © 2005 by Kevin Prufer
All rights reserved
Printed and bound in the United States of America

PENNSYLVANIA
COUNCIL
ON THE
ARTS

10 9 8 7 6 5 4 3 2 1

Contents

Mary

one

Fallen from a Chariot

There is, first of all, her body,
                     and the snow around it
so, at a glance, it is the glittering body of a god who fell
too far
          and can no longer rise, cannot transform—
a bird, a deer—away.

—

The snow, of course, from the trees, with the wind.

Or the car and the bridge it fell from, the rail
that like the body is twisted.
                   The broken windshield
from which the body flew and a hand below the belly,
not a god's hand, but hard as a root,

the other, pointed up as though it could sprout leaves—

—

The zero in the body, the mind that left it
when the face blued and the fingers uncurled
and afterward froze—
                   It is a comfort
that the eyes don't see the snow covering them,
that, finally, only we can move the body away.

—

Good, too, that she precedes us.
Good that we have, as a lesson, her car
which, unlike the body, steams
                    but to us means nothing.
Good to believe that the body is, after all, merely
a machine that has stopped
                   and will not work again.

A Car Has Fallen from a Bridge

There is the death of the car, which was quiet and signifies little, ticking gently in a field of snow.

And there is the death of the body, which was quick, the body unaware and cooling against the dash.

Of course, there is snow, which wants so badly just to sleep, surrounding the car and the body where they came to rest.

How gentle the snow seems from the car, like a gauzy curtain the wind blew from a window on a fall day perhaps years ago. How sweet,

the little paw prints where the sprung glass scattered.

People drive over the bridge not noticing the rail has torn away, not noticing the car that rolled into the field and, moments ago, just died.

I want to be younger than I am.

I want to say to my mother, *no.* To cry in the back seat because I am bored and hungry and we are still one hundred miles from home.

The car lay in the field and the head slept on the dash. An ambulance pulled to the edge of the bridge

but could not figure out how to descend to the frozen field and the car, which was already dead.

Sometimes, I think I understand death, my mother whose heart just stopped while she spoke to a friend on the phone. *Painless, painless,*

I say then. And *merciful,* the receiver dangling from its cord.

How nice to go that way, like a car that one moment is happy and, another, suspended in flight where the bridge broke loose.

To the body, the snow is neither cold nor gentle. To the body, there's a zero where a field should be.

If I only had a cell phone, I would try to call her.

For the Dead: Car Crash

So many have before me, I said,
gone this way. As though I should, therefore, not
be afraid.
    How to sing it? Like a bird might sing me away.
Outside, the car tires crooned, each to each,
through the slush,
      and the bus brakes and the ambulance,
in its siren, a lilting tune. *Oh,* I said from my room
how many stories up,
      don't sing me away.

—

I do not think I said it, though the mind went empty and numb.

So much, in retrospect—the sense
       that now the city lived
as a bird might live on a branch, its heart quick in the
wire ribs—so much that at the time
       was uncertain or absent
entirely. I could not think I was dying when, at last

—

I died. The snow came down. And somewhere, two boys
in a truck, turned wrong
      and kept turning in the sleet,
through the rail and down
      the embankment slope, turned
over and over, while the blond one cried out and the truck stopped
on its side

—

in a scatter of birds lifting up, and up, like a net
pulled taut at the corners, from the trees.
                                        A graceful silence
when the wheels stopped and from under the hood
a final breath of smoke. The birds rose, then drifted away

——

as, later, the ambulance sang to a stop
and the men poured out with their stretchers.
                                        The road
was a silence. The men scrambled down the bank—
and the truck just died. The city, alive; the boys, a comfort and gone;

——

and I, somehow, also. But I could see it,
                                        my hand
placed over my chest.
                        Could see it, when, at last,
someone closed my eyes—

A single bird remained on the branch to watch, crushable
in its feathers and bones,
                        a delightful machine
that could not help but swallow its heart.

An Angel

If memory serves, his wings were crushed and useless—
He plummeted into the road and set the dogs
to barking,
                    eyes turned up to his skull's dull
bowl. *Beautiful,*
                    our children said in their slippers
and gauze, for they had been awakened. They stroked
the wings
                    until sparks glowed beneath their hands.
And his face was dust covered and gorgeous,
a bit of soot at the eyecorners,
                                        a touch of curl
in the lips. We said he was only a body,
and therefore inanimate,
                                        transient and, perhaps,
flammable. We built a ring of stones around him.

As I recall, he was already dead.
                                        It was a hush
of wind that riffled the wings and fluttered
the black eyelashes. A spark
                                        in the nerves, reflexive,
that twitched the wrist or pulsed like blood
in his empty neck and thigh.
                                        Such a body
his soul crawled out of—we couldn't let it stay.
Our children needed sleep, and as for us—
we touched each feather
                                        with gas and flame
until they glowed and shook, one hundred
little index fingers.

An Ambulance

The one asleep in the doorway had snow in her hair.
Quick, quick, the siren called from far away,
but she was quiet as a doll, a bit of ice that would not melt

on her lips. And, for a while, we crowded around,
prodded her with sticks and bits of glass
as though she would unfold her giant wings

and rise away. It was a gentle winter night,
the boys gliding up and down the avenue in perfect cars.
She did not look as old as all that, the cold

having tightened the skin around her eyes and mouth.
I thought to slide my fingers over the whites of her cheeks
to see if they held another breath. The ambulance's wheels

went *hush* against the wet road until they stopped
and flashing lights cast us in a sort of red devil glow.
Stand back, a paramedic said, unfolding a bed,

then lifting her beneath the arms so the tips of her wings
dragged lines across the ground. I thought then
that some things are too sad to be made beautiful.

When they closed the white doors and pulled away
the wheels made fading tracks in the snow.

Tired Old Men Asleep in Their Chairs

Standing they are only belly and spindle legs,
unsteady and vaguely sad,

but asleep in a quiet row of deck chairs
near the crowded pool, glasses put away,

they are so content that a passing girl might laugh
and want to touch their mottled skin

as the sun glances over their cheeks
and startles each white chest.

—

Whether they notice the boys falling
from the high dive concerns no one.

They could sleep all day, hands draped
hotly over their bellies, ice cubes melting

in their drinks. The boys show off
for each other, falling one by one, laughing

into the pool. Every wakeful moment is sad
because the boys don't care for them—but asleep,

—

the smiling old men see a play of soft red light
through closed eyelids. They must be dreaming

about an angel falling
gracelessly to earth, battering himself

so his wings spring from the sockets
and wrench awry, the naked form cooling on cement,

a tanned body that cannot, for all its effort,
find a final breath.

"They Shall Be Left to Fall as They Are Inclined by Their Own Weight"

—Jonathan Edwards

Think of the tight wedge of the seat, the tray-table
unfolded, the stewardess
                              arriving with drinks.

Or of that comfortable space
where wind bends
                              around the airplane's wing.

Nothing is as safe as I want it to be.

Sparks from the wing flaps, smoke in the aisle—
such a sudden shake so the face masks
dropped. A cloud arched past.
                              Like the body,

the craft fell of its own weight,
the cities glittering
                              as the clouds broke.

I have always hoped that if my body resumed
its terrible weight,
                    I would know enough to say:
It is fitting, Lord. It is fitting.

And as my body fell through the sky,
my tie whipping the air behind me:
                              this, too, is just.

I confess a certain weight—

but knew the lord would never drop me
                                      from such a height,
his arms like hulls. But knew—as the airplane

heaved and the clouds rolled by—
a safety. The face masks swayed
                              like vines.

Each wing sheared off
                    so, one by one,
the passengers were blown through the holes.

I held the armrests as though nothing
were the matter,
                  as though, for all my thirty years,
I have been weightless.

Air Disaster Over Kansas

Did a shining god put a kiss on the nose cone?
The airplane rocked on its wings, an engine droned

then coughed. A rotor stopped and would not turn
again. The gas tank burned

and someone saw a creature on the wing
scraping long talons over the singed

flaps, gray head tucked low. I drained
my drink and called the stewardess. *The plane,*

she said, *is going down. Will you have a last
and final scotch?* I would. I gave her all my cash

for which she thanked me, backing queasily
away. The others sat uneasily

craning their dull necks to the windows
as the hungry creature bit the wing. Although

it was little comfort, it occurred to me
through the stink of smoke and gasoline,

that America loves a doomed and falling
populace as much as it loves anything.

Dissected Bird

The heart comes out of the rib cage.

A small collapse of lungs, grown hard and curved like fingernails,
     comes out of the breast.

Pick the stomach from the belly's clot.

Tweeze seeds from the stomach, if you must.

Each wing reveals a socket, hollow as a skull. Scrape them clean of chaff.

Though you say they live in sockets, the eyes come out of holes,

which, emptied, are sad to look at—little caves for bugs.

A breath came from it once, invisibly and quick.

A beat and a call. An egg or a burst of flight from the wings, a tuck
     from the legs.

There is a song for the liver and one for the spleen. A tune for
     every thing.

A rustling of wings where the soul once lived, a scratching as if wanting

out and into the sky, sweet bird, red bird—youth

and the ache that goes with it. Wings like dead leaves,

the twisted fist of the head, a beak to make the fingers bleed,

a feather to write your name.

two

My Life with Caesar

When I was a child, my father and I would wait by the river
for the blue heron that came, each afternoon, to feed.

Creak of a board in the old dock, churn of the water that pushed
a moored boat to the planks—I cannot purify myself

of earthly memories. In a shower of feathers, the heron descended
to the bank, legs unfolding like paper clips, head nodding

on a stem. Once I sneaked close enough to see
its eyes were black and ringed with red. From the cave of his skull

a wind rustled the grass tips until they bowed.

—

The gorgeous obedience of the grass, tips like chins to the ground,
the whisper of feathers as the moon came up—*There is no other king*

than Caesar, no other. Now, when I hear him come, I row my coffin
alone to his shore and kneel on the bank where his footprints are.

Caesar plucks fish from the river, his beak entering the water
in a cloud of spray. As I watch, my throat is tight with eggs,

my cupped hands overflow. *When will the hatchlings sing?*
I ought to ask. Caesar is a breath through the trees,

a sigh from the docks. I do not have a voice to please him.

The Rise of Rome

Rose like a fog off a lake at dawn as the bus rolled past, a young man nodding sleepily against the glass.

Rose from the runway like an airplane that has not long to live.

Rise, the pastor told us, and we rose from our pews and fingered the books because we knew

our time was short. We sang and bowed our heads, then kneeled.

It was a gorgeous empire in its brick and marble. Gorgeous,

like a new car, all windshield and chrome. I wanted to touch it, to slide my finger along the headlight's bee-eye of glass

and not think about it overturned in a field, the wheels slowing and the cockpit just smoke.

Rise, the gods said in their wisdom and rings. *Rise,* in their fingers nettled over with scars, in their whimsical and gratuitous

anger and love. Rome rose and rose like a fog

and we said *yes* to the gods and played our guitars. *Yes* and boarded our planes, or drove the long roads outside of the city

where the sun came down and no one plowed it away. It was a marvelous time,

faster and faster like smoke. The baths and the aqueduct, the opulent quarter and the less

opulent. I swam in perfume while my servants ate mice, while the borders collapsed and planes crowded the skies. *Oh give me, give me,* I said to the gods who grinned around their crystal balls.

It was always summer while Rome was rising. The pastor said *kneel.* The gods just laughed.

We spread our beach towels on the sand and collapsed.

Poor Hannibal of Carthage

No one wanted him in the ballroom with the drinks.
The stewards gave him such a look that said, *Poor Credit* or *Stain*,
said, *You have lost us the Empire*
                            with all this dithering.

And Julia who wouldn't speak to him, but smiled up at the band.

So out to the cruise ship's stern where he could smoke
and ash his cigarette into the sea.

—

And the sparks were orange and lovely spinning into waves.
Slap of sea against the steel hull,
                            call of a seagull and the spring and fall
of Julia laughing at some rich man's joke.

—

He'd banged his head against it and Rome wouldn't fall. He'd kicked it
and thrown his shoulder out against the stones,
                            but no.

Over the walls with a torch and a bomb, over the walls
with the bodies of peasants and into the street, but Rome like a tank—

or Rome like a smile—kept grinding away.
                            The stewards said *No*
and moved to the other side of the room with the drinks.
The women smiled politely or shook their heads,

and even Julia, who'd been laughing a moment ago

—

gave him such a look with narrowed eyes that what could he do,
having brought his elephants over the Alps and to the sea,

having brought his men against the legions and up to the gates?

He'd shoveled the frozen and the stiff away
                                          and dropped them
from the cliffs. He'd eaten the hoofs of ice-cold horses
and touched the walls of Rome,

—

had touched the very gates, then hurled a burning peasant's body
over the crenellations and into the street.
                              From far away,
he heard them laughing, the ice that sang in their drinks,
the ship's band playing such a tune that wafted on the breezes
like contagion.
                    And Julia dancing in her ball gown,
arms around another man,
                              and the dull sweep
of light through the portholes and over the deck.

—

All the way from Carthage and up the Spanish coast.
                                          Through camps
where old men tended dying flames. Gaul and the Arverni,
                                          and still
he couldn't have a drink or some thin woman's hips against him.
He dropped his cigarette into the sea. *Failure,*

—

failure, the women said, turning away. And, *Sorry, old boy,*
from their dates, stirring their drinks and calling to the band.
And even the stewards
           who should have carried him in a golden box, said *No,*
as though he were a germ

—

or a loss. Rome still standing.
                      Rome in its lovely dress of blue lights,
Rome in its lipstick and its pearls, Rome in its laughter and lilac
perfume,
           in the arms of another, her breath upon his cheek
while the ship moved on to a freezing island
                                       he never chose to see.

The Historian's Prayer to the Deified Augustus

It was the thirty-ninth year of a troubled reign.
You'd ordered closed the gates to signify a peace,
then, draped and old in bed, you died.

The fig trees bent and dripped in the rain-soaked field.
A hand brushed the pillow, a god's. Your face,
as those on coins, smoothed over—then, finally

unreadable. Trick from an old text. I always wanted
a brittle note to hinge from the pages into my palm
like a last breath. Like truth. I don't know what to do

with history's stare—so always, at night,
the lamp turns dull on the page. A lure from a window,
the strange war of crickets high in trees—listen,

won't you call the stars down to kiss the grass?
To lick dew from the grass with their pointed tongues?
Won't you glide to earth and hold your wings just so?

As if to say, *Here I am, come from heaven?*

The Death of Augustus

When he would not eat what was served him, Livia poisoned the figs on the trees.

Came to him in old age like flowers in the mail
unexpected and sweet
                    but mottled where the leaves curled
where the leaves could wilt away

Come lovely he said Come gorgeous in your pot of blue
Come like a lily that drifts in a pool when the sea recedes

and a cool wind kisses the sand into rivulets He did not care

—

He did not know a thing He'd been asleep for years
A hand from the clouds pulled him from his feather bed
to the sky
              the hand that plucked the garden bare
that touched the figs on their branch That killed the branch
That brought a single poison fig
                              to his lips That held it in his mouth
like an ache

—

A voice from the cloud said goodbye The ache in the throat said
feed me The fat horse tethered to the fence asked why? clopping
its hooves in the dirt
                    but he was gone away he had gone
and his Forum grew over The statues wilted on each pedestal
so the sky like a wheeze A throat The suck of breath

—

before the gasp

—

and the snows began   The horse fell onto its side and slept
and did not rise when the wind ruffled its mane

Did not rise when it blew snow against its back
and buried it
                    stiffening its legs its neck arched in sleep

—

Finally the great must—all of them—
                                        So Augustus
put the poison fig to his lips to taste and fell
back in his bed so his soul was lifted away

A hand from the blue squall of sky   The sea
crying over its beach   A flower
                                    each petal twisting
from the branch   The empire slipped with a cough then a gasp

Fell loose-jawed   Fell slack
                        alone and asleep

Caligula, Clairvoyant

The punctured skullplate
                    opened nicely. The surgeons tweezed it up
then dropped it on the table like a saucer. Blood clot, clump
of blondish hair—his head was a hole in a dome. Caligula
bit his tongue while the surgeons poured a poison
                                        on his brain
and sewed the skullplate back.

—

Such a headache, then, to turn birds into pains in the trees.
Such a grisly thrill, the sun with its muddy fingers
drumming on the sill. So he walked the streets at night
                                        past Nubians
and their funny wagonloads of lime, the empty public baths, to the bars
where he could be anyone in a corner—

—

Like bombs, the wobbling of cups in saucers, like little deco starbursts.
No wonder he turned mean
                    and exhausted. The surgeons in their wealthy
villas, looking over the Esquilline toward the sea. The surgeons
with their scalpels and remote control,
                            their pudgy oyster faces.
No wonder Caligula became a god.

—

And over the city, an airplane thrummed and swagged, low
as a migraine with its trail of bombs—
                    In the park,
he watched a peculiar young man hide under a bench as,

one by one, the buildings shook and died,
                              as the fields outside Rome
burned like blankets on which a cigarette has fallen

—

The poison under the skullplate turned like a gray cloud
so the future was a searing in the eyes, so Rome was a wasp's nest
of motorbikes and noise, of cafés
                              and boys in aprons balancing drinks
upon their trays, of airplanes that opened like milkweed pods
scattering their seeds over the last of the city.

—

And under the park bench, the shadow of the man
looked toward the ruins of the square, where the cafés had closed,
the umbrellas folded away—
                              It was a lovely city,
in its gold coins and arches, splendid where the fires
spread up the walls like vines.
                              Triple exposure, rot
where the dulled brain died. And distance
                              made a drama of it.

Caligula on Death

His ghost haunted the gardens until he was given a proper burial.

They put a dagger in my gut then threw me in a cart
and left me at the city's edge.

I slept in a tumble of roots, hands splayed around my head,
mouth agape.
                    A weed grew between my fingers,
curled around my wrists. My face plate
                                 caved, each eye gone soft,
deflated and strange.

—

In Capri, I thought my uncle died. He looked so calm in his bed.
I kissed his head
                    then eased his golden ring away.
                                      He coughed.

I kissed his head again,
                    then put a pillow to his mouth.

And so his body stilled.

We powdered the syphilitic spots that scarred his royal face,
then put him in a box and carried him to his grave.

Thus he became a god

—

and I became a weed near a path.

First bloomed,
                    then lost my petals to the cold,
                                   then bloomed again.

—

Large eyes, sleep-injected lips, and dry— The properly buried
desire the living
                but cannot speak.

Their mouths like caves and deep.
                          The tongues that sleep.

I have read that it is best
                    to avoid their island,

hands that reach to touch the livings' cloaks,
the questions they would ask—

—

What I wouldn't give—

—

A bird has pecked my eyes away. There are certain things I know,
having read a great deal.

Tiberius dreams of Rome.

I'm often walking blindly through the snow.

—

And it is a sin to bury the dead poorly.
                       I sleep in a tangle of roots,
my coat gone loose at the chest.
                  My uncle in a box,

his shade that skimmed the sea and found the island I shall never find.

Were I to travel there

—

                like Odysseus,
I'd feed him honey and an ox's blood.

I'd look into the hole that was his eye and tell him, *Yes.*
They remember you well.
                    No one scars your coins
or tilts your statues from their blocks into the sea.

I'd smile
         because my smile has served me well.

Claudius Adrift

He is a dullard and he cannot speak.

—Livia

A cracking of the sail against the mast
                    brought me back,
though having nothing to say, I lay on the deck chair and did not move.
The foremast wagged like a finger.
                    The sun
thundered down and, *Oh,* I heard Gracie say from somewhere
below deck, *deal them right! You're dealing them all upside down
and everywhere,* and then they were laughing and someone else said,
get me a drink.
                    Seemed the harbor had drifted off somewhere,

—

seemed it crawled far away as I simmered and browned—
and how elegant with one eye open, how fine
                    the stretch of it,
the smile of masts in the distance, the row of hulls
                    as though
nothing could undo them, no fighter plane to break their planks,

—

and it's true, some god carved out my tongue, replaced it with a fish.
It's true, my fingers shake and my left eye drifts.
I am always opening my mouth to speak
                    having thought great things,
and the others stop talking and smile and wait.
                    Such a patience
and sting until I close my scalèd mouth and leave the room.

—

41

How splendid and sad it was, I wanted to say, when Carthage fell,
each soldier sprinkling the street with salt.

                       And one by one, the windows
grinned into flame. The library swayed on its pillars, groaned
as the roof fell through into glitter and cloud.

I have always loved the grand moment,
the great, abstracted
               dying off, when the city collapses and trees blaze.

—

And, *He is writing a history,* my mother said, *of stammerers and dolts.*
And, *Draw already!* from below. *Draw a card or pass.*

                               Gracie laughed
and, as if from far away, ice chuckled in a glass. Call me no one,
for I'll never inherit. Call me lovely, because I have failed.

—

                       And far away, Rome slept
in its bed, Rome was dying and how badly
                    I wanted to make a poem
of it, wanted poor Valerian skinned again, wanted Julian
speared by his troops then carried back home, or Nero
stabbed while his guards ran off
                and the city just burned.

—

I am a young man now, but when I grow old,
                    my duplicitous wife
will bring me dinner. She will smile and look out the window
toward the boats and the harbor. I will eat a mushroom
and fall from my chair.

Beautiful Nero

"What an artist the world is losing!"

We'd made such a day of it—
until the sun fell behind the trees and the streetlamps came awake.

We drank and sang
            and old Paula fell out of her chair into the street
while Wilson spilled my drink, then called the waitress with the sponge.

And then the boys were dragging café tables inside for the night,
the metal legs scraping the pavement white
                        Good night, Irene, good night,
I called into the air. And *Drink up!* Paula said, *Drink up!*
laughing and opening her purse.

And then I was alone and had to find another place to sit.

—

In the back of my throat, some god once burned a song. *How beautiful,*
my mother said when, as a boy, I opened my mouth to sing. *Lovely,*

lovely. A blister and a scar—
                   Like Nero, I can't help but add a trill
to any bit of paper caught and fluttering down the street,
or the cat slipping past on a blur of legs.
                       And *Oh!* she said, when
at the piano the silver thread of my voice unrolled.

—

The night Rome burned, Nero sang. *Yes,* the lyre told him, and he played,
perched on the balcony.
                   Sing, the city said in its embers,
and Nero sang. And the buckets of water, passed hand-to-hand below
called *More!* and the girls in the street, their gowns burning so gently

up their bodies, clapped, *Bravo!* while all at once the library heaved
and crumbled,
               fell in upon itself and died. And *Beauty,* Nero said
under his breath, his hands stopped on the lyre, his face orange
in the smoke-filled light.

—

Years later the bombers came like little black notes over the city,
like trills.

Yes, I lost the song in my throat, but crouched in the park
beneath a tree, hands over my head, and cried

thinking of no one but myself while the deep-voiced bombs called
one building after another into the ground

and all at once a treetop bloomed in flame.

—

I sat in the park and sang
                  as Paula and Wilson staggered home,
while across the road the café owners turned out their lights.
Lovely, lovely, I remembered my mother saying, *it's beautiful,*

clapping her hands from the living room when I was through.
Beautiful, I thought, leaning back on the park bench
while the city dozed and the lights went out on such music,

the ache in my throat, a quiet evening.

—

In the end, Nero could not do the job,
                    but cried for his slave to finish
him off. And from the ashes of Rome, the troops approached
so he could hear their horns and boots.
                    Always, a scar where a god
burned a song. How lovely, when a city dies
and one is far enough away to make a song of it.

I sat in the park and sang.
                    The city crouched in a darkness.
And then, the slave said, *Yes,* drawing his blade.

Roman Economics

God came out of the sky with his golden fingers

and the Romans
never knew it. *Sleep, sleep now,* he said

swagging his magic watch on a chain,
I will count to ten,

but the Romans didn't hear him,
engrossed in their commerce and public baths, wrapped in their togas
with the purple hems.

—

A bird reclined on the arch of Titus, and the people said, *A sign!*
A bird lay on its back and died on Trajan's Column,

and they said,
It will be bad for us on the Danube.

The tribes will paint their faces
with all our ground-up taxes.

And God just waved his watch
above their heads, said, *Sleep, sleep,*

said, *Lo, a Day will come*
when you look into the Watch Spring and know your Time is past—

—

which the Romans never minded.
Commerce was a pastime and the downfall

of the citizenry,
who lolled in the gardens at the Forum's center.

The senator slept in the glorious golden box
on the shoulders of eleven healthy slaves.

The emperor napped in his ivory bed and scrolls.

—

The watch chain slipped over the city like lightning and God said, *Rain!*
And the Romans, lacking umbrellas, ducked into the many shops.
God said, *Hear me!*
God said, *Look!* Said, *Lend me your Ears!*
And the storm accosted the paving like coinage.

The live bird rose from the arch of Titus and the dead one
slept in a puddle.
The watch ticked on its chain,
but who could read it? Not the Romans, who loved the lukewarm air
of the tepidarium,
who sank, one by one, into the elegant baths.

Lives of the Later Caesars

They fell from their trees like dying leaves caught in a cold wind—
    into the street, over the park, trapped in a gust and away.

Or they fell like a train from a bridge, one by one the cars going
    under.

One pushed from a tower into the yard, where he lay unsocketed
    and no one would drag him away.

Into the Nile, into the Tiber. Into a plastic bag like a kitten, and
    knotted. So down and down they sank

to where their heels dug into the river bottom and no one could find
    them again.

One choked on a peach, one used for a footstool by the Persian
    king, one gutted and boned and worn as a cloak—

Sometimes, eating a piece of cake on the balcony, I think, How
    proud

the long string of them, like flawed and lovely pearls. How fine they
    might have been, were they not

fat-fingered and vulgar, were they not duplicitous, half-drunk, and sad.

A bit of cake is nice in the evening when the sun slides over New
    York like a yellow peach and the people are home and watching TV.

Now and then, a grid of birds rises from the park like a black net
    and into the dying sun.

At such times I think we will never fall, our buildings firm as a
    gladiator's armored shins.

The Fall of the Roman Empire

When the lights go out on a peaceful evening, it is wartime.
Who pulled the switch? Sometimes
                              all he heard was water
on sand and even the ship lights flickered off, the bulbs
swaying emptily on their poles.
                              The bombers always rose
from the horizon invisibly after dark.

He dropped a glass of wine. A bloodied handprint
on the sand. The boats sighed on their mooring,
their fine wood scraping the docks.
                              He didn't think
any bombers were coming.

—

Gracie and Earl and James. Paula and Wilson. A cloud
fell over the town and into his lungs. *Blow wind, blow,*
he was singing,
                  but couldn't remember the words.
Some of his friends at their windows looked to the sky
for bombers. Some in the fields, hands crooked or splayed,
faces damp from rain.
                  There was no one to bring them in.

The beach was tranquil at night, as though he had never seen
a falling bomb.
            Lawn dart, dropped bottle, bad word.

Never seen one tilt into the sand, but heard them
grumbling on the distant islands.

—

When Rome fell, the Romans never knew it. No one burned
the buildings down.
                    Weeds, of course, in the Forum.
A roof and no one to clear the tiles away.

Not like a bomb, not like a president. Not like the market,
ratings, the cost of gas. A sun kept rising. The same old gods
laughed up their sleeves.

A woman stopped for the night in a ruined farmhouse,
unrolled her mat, and slept.
                    Her brooch slipped into the rubble
so she could not find it the next day.

—

Dew collects at the eyecorners and slides down the face
when one is dead in a field. Of course, the eyes don't see.

The lights went out in town
                    and nothing to look at, anyway.

The bombers were unimportant to the passed-away,
                    his friends
who remembered a Christmas long ago, a shrill wind
scattering snow beneath the door and into the living room.

—

Such snow, his mother said, sweeping it with a broom into the corner,
then blocking the space under the door with a towel. He looked up
from his book. The room smelled of pine and hearth. It was a book
about the fall of Rome. A wind laughed over the house

played its fin-
gers on the chimney so sleepily and trim that he would close his eyes
on the sofa in front of the fire, he would put down his book, and,
although it wasn't time for sleep, he would shut them, his eyes, his
book, shut them away.

—

Some of them may have thought it. It was centuries ago.
A few, perhaps, in ruined temples. A few, in their boots,
beneath the standards.
                    Five soldiers straggled back into town,
grieving and tattered. Illyricum, Parthia,
the wrong side of the Danube.
                    A bit of dirt in the duffel,
strange implement, beer.

More birds in Rome than people. Some couldn't help noticing
the sparrow that came to rest on the arch of Trajan,
how it did not move all day
                    then, during the night,
just vanished.

—

Rome died. A Christmas, long ago, he had been reading about it,
and now, how strange the words were. *Alaric,* like a catch in the
throat. *Honorius,* the smooth ache in the back of the mouth. And
his wine spilled and his friends in their rooms looking for bombers.
His friends in the fields, streaked with dew.

—

And then it rained and he jogged back toward the villa,
dropping his wine on the sand.

He had had too much.
The waves came in and in, and, from far away,
the throb of an airplane's motor.

How strange when it came low over the beach,
and he fell into the brush, cupped his hands over his ears.
A whistle
        of bombs. Unbearable. The tall grass swayed
around him, touched his cheek. Such an itch.
                                    Such snow,
his mother had said. *Such snow. See it coming down, so gently?*
Into the woods. Over the Forum.
                        It was a terrific snowstorm,
they all agreed. Such a crash and a roar. Into the lap of God.

Ode to Rome

The poem about the fall of Rome
drops stones in my water glass.
                There is an ache in the back of my throat.
The poem about Rome has a shell in its beak,
it feeds my ear, is what my ear
                      asks for. Here is the end

of Rome in a pasta dish. Here, the last of the buildings
on a silver fork, the last
                of the street lamps
in the sugar in the well of a coffee cup. When the sun sets

and the poem, on its nest in the dark,
                    adjusts its bird eyes
my throat contracts. A thousand winters where the grass grew
over the avenues. A litter of statues.

Without cities,
                I don't know what to say to myself, I cannot
whisper my ear to sleep.
                The ode to Rome
is a whimper of feathers, a scurry of black wings.

Goodbye to the City, We Have No Other

We have no other king but Caesar.
We have no other bread than what he places on our dry tongues.

Our bodies are always dissolving.
The golden armbands went missing from the caves. *Quick, quick,*

a woman was heard to say. *We must write down all our thoughts*
and hide them in clay pots. We must bury the pots in loam

where they will keep. We have no other wind
than that which whips our faces red. We have no other fears

than this: The sky darkening to a close like a great black moth,
the collapse of many-veined wings.

We are years on years, and count our dead in leaves.
We say it now, in retrospect: We have no other king,

had no other—even when the elms skittered into spring,
when cobbles wore our footsoles thin—

we had no other king but Caesar.

three

Youth and the Lie That Goes with It

The youth in the onion's core
and the sprung shoot
that digests it
         so the skin
slackens and the center grows
soft
      as an old man who says,
Wasn't it sweet? Back then,
an old man settling into a soft chair,
It was lovely,
        then gone,
as the TV sleeps and the books
say nothing.
         It was good times,
his legs on the table, drink in hand,
laughing,
         while in the kitchen
the little lie,
         the shoot
from the center of the onion,
eats its core.

Poem for My Mother at Her Age

Stars are one thing we never run out of,
the way they fill the black air with a million little breaths.
Look at them, you said from the lawn furniture
meaning the hands that smeared the stars above the house.
And, just as suddenly, the memory of a pulp of lightning bugs
that set my arms and face to glittering—it was a long time ago
that night came down like a colander over the neighborhood
and you turned the house lights on to keep the dark away.

Narcissistic Elegy

The little black gun where my heart should be
                                        fired and fired until,
like yours, it stopped. And such a pause in my chest,
my ribs grown steel and the cave all dark, grown barred—
                                        The hammer
clicked and the gun just sparked.

—

And the trees in the window went *whoosh* in the wind,
and my little black gun was dead, like yours—
                                        How strange! And grim
as the snow came down so the wind blew white
like a hospital's room, as white as your sickroom—
                                        Soon and *soon*

—

but your breath wouldn't come. *Oh soon,* I said,
but no breath in the room.
                        And the books on the nightstand
and the nurse call box—I watched your chest but it never rose,
and I watched your chest, but the room now quiet
as the breathless awe
                when the guns all stop and the hero dies.

In the End the Doorbells Stop

In the end the doorbells stop   and the useless animals
curl under the houses   paws to their chins.

We will not have mouths   to call them out
or hands to smooth their fur.

In the end the radios lose   their clatter   static
and spit   airwaves fuzzy headed   and gone.

We will not have lips to touch   another's eyes.

In the end the sun goes down   like the last of Rome
with a sigh.

—

There will be birds in a few years   simmering
over the street   scattering the lawns with silver seeds.

For a while the screen doors   might slam in the wind

There will be leaves   as there now are   on the trees.

Snow will continue   to sift into my eyes   fill my eyes
or rain like hot glass   or wind.

There will be dollar bills   but they will not keep
pulping in the box   as we sleep our last.

Old Woman

Someone unfastened the moorings
so the ship slipped out to sea.

Silly vessel, a grind of empty ribs
and sway of flags—

I watched it drift away,

a gentle cough in the masts
where the slack ropes slapped the joists,

where the loose sails blew—

It was like an old woman, aimless
and pleased with herself, unknotted

and free while the last sun heaved.
Where was it going?

It laughed at the waves

then turned in a current, its boards
grown loose with rot.

When the daylight died for good,
I lost it in the black.

The Dead in Their Boats

When a flood undid the cemetery grounds
each coffin floated off,

the dead drifting gratefully downriver.

And some rowed their coffins swiftly,
calling to one another across the angry water's swath,

throwing their pointless rings and charms into the air.

And some just sang, looking raggedly before them
at the trees.

—

How glare where an armbone broke the skin,
how curled in the flesh-flap, dried away in the night's hot air.

Lush, as the mourning left them—in their dress-up suits, in boxes.

Or cured like a leaf and brittle in the carton,
looking up at the stars and smiling.

Some dead rowed and others leaned back
to love the warm fall wind.

—

For years, each rain washed mud between their slats
and streaked the aching faces—

For years, in their envelopes underground—

So strange and drug to come upon them now. So grim,
the dead awash in wooden boats, splashing the water up.

—

I stood on the shore and watched them pass, the moonlight
catching their brittle bones and hair—and almost

wanted to laugh along, having lost loved ones, too,
like anyone—

and almost to sing the same drunk song as they,
rowing their coffins down dull flood waters

and happily into sea.

Burial at Sea

It is, perhaps, not empty. Inside
the dulled heart might still, in its package, quake.
The body is not like a shell

after the sea has rolled the dying flesh away,
it is not a shell washed in the surf or bleached
a helpless white. One cannot tell

what lives inside when the arms grow slack,
when the eyes won't wake. Someone
rolled it from the ship and into the sea

so the body turns in the waves and seems,
at times, to sink— But who can say
what the head thinks? And the ship,

as it sails, the young girls throwing rose petals
from the stern so they trail in the sea—
And the mast that groans in its joists

as the ship retreats, the sailor's one-note
song— They are, we say, only proper oblation
for a body that drifts

impossibly far from the rest of us.

A Gull in the Water

First the wings went slack against the body.
The motor collapsed in the breast.
Beak and claw and eye—like dead technology.
A wind detached one feather from the rest
and tossed it to the docks
where men unwound their lines into the sea.
The gull revolved in the surf and rocked
where the waves rushed in. Poor species
of delight, a semblance of the free—
its eyes glazed white, its legs like disconnected
wires—the gull appeared to be
content to float where the tides intended,
to relax the tension of wing and cry,
a machine that could drift but wouldn't fly.

Questions for the Drowned at Sea

Are you loose and vague as a sea grown still
after rain? Or cool as salt water when the season's
fall, when the sun is low and the air is chill?
Can you move? Do you say
I try, but my legs won't kick? I had my looks,
but they've gone away?

Can you swim? Are you closer, now, to a fish,
your mind all dumb and your head just float?
Or to a raft, in the water's clasp, in the random swish
and turn? How odd,
in the wide expanse where the water yawns
at the shore. What god

swam off with your ghost? Did he stuff it in a bottle
and give it to the winds and the sea
so its ink's gone smeared and the message is a muddle
of blue? Will it roll
in the surf or dry on the sands of the beach?
Are you vessel? Or soul?

Lily

How does the body contain so much blood?
The brain sleeps in it

—

so when we bleed we lose ourselves.

—

The brain under its curved sky of bone, the brain that turns on its stem
like a waterlily.

—

A cluster of leaves and bloom, a hum of flies. The day retards
into dusk. Horsefly, dragonfly,

—

a dull thrum of clear wings against the ear. What is their language?
I want my hands to flex when the doctor stings them.

—

I want to open my mouth and speak.

—

It is either a long and mindless sleep
or a translation into a language I do not know.

—

The blood that washes the brain to sleep. The wings that rest
on the unfurled petal. Divine translation, strange word, insect

—

where the soul should be.

About the Dead

What is important about the dead is their absence.

It doesn't matter what they're thinking
nor how stiff their dying suits have grown.

Their arms are heavy and the air is gone,
the dead tucked noiselessly
                              into envelopes of earth,

—

though sometimes they may pity us,
                              our immortal souls
lashed to tall masts, floating downriver,

our souls in these terrified animal bodies,
all muzzle and cry, tied up.

—

I can only tell my skill-less life floatingly
and from afar,
                on a weak wind.

I have always wanted beauty
                              to come like a word
from the dead—the cattails along the riverbank bursting
their transient white seeds,

—

or the heron, a cold wind in its tired skull,
lifting, suddenly, away—it is the dead

who describe themselves too gorgeously
as if to say
            the very best moment comes when we leave.

four

The Empire in the Air

It was a fragile empire
with knobs and wires, like a bomb.
It lived in a blue suitcase in the airplane's belly.
It had a little screen that flashed the time
and the moments we had left, ticked them gently away.
We laughed and sipped our drinks
while the empire, wrapped in its inevitable wires,
imagined the airplane splitting like a milkweed pod,
the clothing that would burst from our broken suitcases
into the air.

The Empire Was Falling

The rains were many and our days were few.
People kept leaping out of windows.

The air was full of businessmen,
their red ties streaming behind their necks.

Dear Editor, I wrote, before I deleted the words.
Dear Editor, We've failed in too many ways . . .

The vines grew long. What cars there were
gasped in the nubs where the alleys ended.

The empire fell through the thickening trees.
Because there was nowhere for them to go,

the crows built a nest in my empty belly
until all I could think was, What shall I do

with my plentiful riches and hoard of tools?
What shall I do with the blades in my heart?

My air was thin, the trees aghast,
draping their branches where the statues drooped.

Each night, I wished the clouds would part.
How could I not desire the stars,

their points obliterating tender thoughts?
But when the weather finally broke

and the crowds stopped scuffling
in the glass-strewn alleys,

each star threw down its pointed leaves
over the empty roofs of the city.

Prayer

What shall I do if I never can reach him?
The bed is a harlot, all laughter and lace.
My teeth like a riot of bridges and gold
so how can he hear me? And what should I say?

The asters and poppies just die in the window,
the rose on its stem is bald where it aches.
The blood fruit rolled from the table then burst,
so how can I kneel, and whom should I face?

The Lord must be sleeping. The bones in my tongue
are rib-like and caught, my mouth is amazed—
but how should I sing and what shall I call him?
He hasn't a name. I don't know his grace.

For the Dead: Unveiling

That my death brought with it
$\qquad$ no sigh beyond the palette
unnerved me.
$\qquad$ *Lord,* I said, *aren't you in the room?*
It seemed an empty room. I died;
$\qquad$ the breaths of those

—

standing over my bed stopped. And such a slack-limbed
sense came
$\qquad$ until, *yes,* I said, *I am a portrait in oils*
over which the artist has drawn a heavy cloth and—

one, two, three—has pulled the cloth away
$\qquad$ as if to unveil
the afterlife to me, as if to unveil me

—

to it. And I don't know what I expected—a landscape, yes
cherubic and done up
$\qquad$ in greens, a sky so low and fast
to excellent weather
$\qquad$ as a catch comes quick
to the throat of one who has watched another die,

that kind of weather.

—

I wanted a god in the room. I wanted, beyond the curtain,
a deep voice.
$\qquad$ I wanted a *yes* and a *no.* A *good. It is done.*
An otherworldly

voice to say I had been, despite it all, worthwhile and,

in places, beautiful. Worthy of

—

a frame. Couldn't I be a portrait
looking at a perfect landscape?
                    The room was silent.
No one said *ah.*
                    No godlike hand unveiled my face.

Final Instructions

Be shot in the chest with an arrow. Then fall.
Be blue where the fingers end, under the nails.

Be pierced
in the cage where the heart once was, then fierce

and dumb while the bowstring
sputters. Nothing

should rattle the heart's bars. Be dead—
that, too. In the snow. Just melt where the body ends

and the drift begins. Or freeze, as the body cools
and the air takes over. How drunk I hope it feels,

how chill in the landscape's wrap of snow.

—

Smile when the shade comes on
and on. Don't bleed or double over. Be gone

in a sigh or a cough. First you'll be alive
and we'll all say, *Faith.* Say, *Believe*

and that will take you. Then the arrow, clean
to the heart, so we can cover you up. Don't scream

or tell us how it hurts. Don't pull the sheet
from your eyes and gaze at the sun. Be neat

about it, so we won't have to think. Smile
and roll your eyes up into your skull

as though there were a heaven that waits for us all.

The Gladiator

When I died
When my blood feathered away and I stared blankly and sideways
into the grass. When the grass ceased
against my cheek, I could not help
but remember the gladiator who, in falling, never groans,
who, ordered to accept it,
does not contract his neck for the final blow.
And the hillside grew quiet. The bombers passed
withering the trees and the city with flame. The empire
fell. My empire, like a blood drop into the grass.
It is of little consequence to the observer
if the gladiator falls forward into the dirt. He is of a mind, merely,
to do as he is told. He will not see the emperor's thumbs.
His city fell to its knees and burned, rolled on its side,
but he won't think of it. Those who once cheered for him
are cheering still. The airplanes
flew over the hill and I, crouched in the grass, was terrified
but did not look up, did not complain
when a last bomb startled me away.

Underground Mausoleum

A hole opened up and a girl fell through

But the bombs kept falling, and I, face down in beach grass,
felt my fingers clench a final time around what in that moment
I mistook for a young girl's hair—
                            such a delight, the sting in my thigh,
the handful of grass, and the fading

music I thought was planes singing the sky to pieces overhead.

—

And remembered a girl I read about who walking in tall grass
slipped into a hole and down,
                            her skirt blown out and floral
until she landed in the underground, forgotten
mausoleum. How pretty, like a wisp, a blown and distant
trumpet, curled and white
                            on the ground, a lightshaft above,
such markings on the walls, indistinguishable. Her legs were broken.

—

The chord of bombers overhead, and she, below,
                            her skirt around her.

I did not know where the music of the planes was taking me
as, in the distance, the town cried into flame, and I, in the grass

by the shore, and the water leaking over and through. A lock of grass
in my palm.

—

Bones of sheep and dogs that vanished through the hole.
And in their carved-out niches, the remains of others,
hands folded over their chests, or wrapped.

Such snow, the dead sing
to the girl, curled and stunned in her white dress. *Down and down.*
The bombs are down and down.

And the girl—I couldn't help imagining,
I couldn't take myself away, my own legs unmoving

and deranged in the grass—

—

and the girl, underground, where she'd fallen, among the bones
of the forgotten, of a flock. And those in their niches, speaking.
We are not, they tell her, *what we once were.*

*We have slipped
so gently into quiet.* They cannot help but love a girl

—

the way they cannot help but love any event.

And it was good when,
after they passed, thieves stole their rings. And it was good when
every lamb fell through the hole.

And the rumble of the plow above
trembled the dead on every ledge. And now

—

with the rain and the bombs, such a time
the long-dead have of it, who cannot remember
                                      why they died,
who have no rings. The girl weeps on the floor, so they tell her,
beauty, beauty. This is what—

—

while she cannot move her legs.
While, above, the fields burned, the houses sighed,
and I could not remove myself from the grass.
                          As I died, the bombs

—

blew shaft after shaft of light
                      over the bones of those speaking.

Lemure

A Roman ghost of an ancestor

Since I came back to this world without a halo to see by,

since I have no choice but to stumble, since I thought that we'd progressed.

My hands are stiff, clasped this way at my chest. My heavy feet, my lashes still falling from my eyes like petals.

When the sentries came, centuries ago, I cried into my sleeve until even the flies abandoned me.

And when they dragged me off, I could not forgive them, but clawed at their forearms, my feet scraping the earth.

Treason, the crowds in the Forum cried. And, *death.* So they put me in a bag, and the bag into the river, where I remained

until fished out. Until pulled from and up the bank, where they untied me and washed my chest and broke my bones

into place so I would look at peace and restful. And they put me in a tomb.

And it was treason, but I could not say no to it. And it was true, but I was not ashamed, being too cold. Since it was gold that I was offered.

In breaths, I have measured every year. And, recently, in plows and bombs on the field above my tomb.

The plow goes overhead like an excellent idea, fading when it reaches the corners of the field, then rumbling back.

Such footsteps, we said of the bombs. *Such legs they have!*

Since there was nowhere else for me to go, I sought you out. Since you have ignored me—

The field is peaceful now that the bombs have stopped. The city smolders on the hill

and a little god keeps singing in the trees.

Who Are Our Barbarians?

The brain in the ATM, and the juice-slick fingers
that flick the money out.
                           The card swipe, the thought
in the magnetic strip, a sad music
                               somewhere
inside the machine
                       singing my numbers away.

—

Or disease like an orange in the mouth,
                               the thrill of the peel
grating the teeth.
                   Sickness a tang and a sorrow
when I read the papers, numbers
                           like petals from a tree.
At a tropical border,
                   no one I know
                               dies in his bed.

—

Neither do I know a soul in prison,
grizzled in black & white,
                       one out-of-focus hand
holding up a name and number, a fruit
where the mind should be.
                       What did he say
in that slurry speech,
                   and where did he come from?

—

When the empire fell,
                    the internet closed
like a refrigerator door. Where were the borders?
I was afraid to start my car—someone
put a mind in the engine.
                              I was afraid
to answer the phone,
                    of the mean little heart
that beat in the mouthpiece.

Apocalyptic Prayer

Please, with your hands, for the warmth
and Please, on the backs of my ears
                                        where they froze.
But the city was a ruin and a mystery,
the cafés closed long ago, their yellow eyes
gone black and still,
                        the bricks caved in.
And a fire, will you start it? Please, with a match
or a lighter. With a flint, which you might
strike on a brick.
                        But the cars were dead on their empty tires,
their needles on zero and still. The bridge folded
and the grass grown wild—
                        Won't you build the city up
with clay or with sticks? Put a fire in the lampposts
so we can see?
                        Only silence from the church
where the steeple was. And silence from the vaults
where the old coins glowed.

I Was the Last Man on Earth

Wonderful that they are all resurrected—the man,
coat sleeves flaming down his arms, the elderly woman
and her steaming footprints in the sidewalk,

the girl, charred matchsticks falling from her school bag.
Wonderful and aimless, but must they be judged
immediately? I was the last man on earth. The pestilence

didn't want me, and neither did the ice, sleeping
across the continent, receding into the cracks.
I moved into a fantastic room pierced by sunlight

twice each day, gathered treasures such as no man
has often seen: emeralds big as fists, banknotes,
pulpy and useless from the meltwater. And now, as was foretold,

abruptly, the others reappear. I've missed them so.
The homeless char the same old doorsteps,
shirts smoldering from their bodies. Must they be judged

and removed so soon? And what about my bracelets, this wallet
these porcelain figurines? When God splits the earth
to take the others back, should I turn the lights off,

leave the jewels? Should I, guilty, descend the stairs
and stand by that crack at the edge of the city?